By Bill Adler

THE JOHNSON
HUMOR

Edited by Bill Adler

Simon and Schuster
New York

CONTENTS

THE JOHNSON HUMOR

Lyndon Baines Johnson has a rare and delightful sense of humor.

He is a gifted storyteller and enjoys entertaining his friends and family with wonderful yarns from his Texas boyhood. Many of his stories are classics of American folk humor.

The thirty-sixth President of the United States has a sharp and ready wit which he has demonstrated in press conferences, on the floor of the United States Senate, on the campaign trail and in off-the-cuff conversations.

The awesome pressures of the toughest job in the world have not dimmed Lyndon Johnson's zest for a good joke, a funny story or a meaningful witticism.

The editor's job has been a joyous one, for from the material in this book emerges a man and President who truly enjoys the sound of laughter.

Bill Adler
New York City

FAMOUS
JOHNSON
STORIES

President Lyndon Johnson told a group of business leaders the following anecdote to explain why large funds were necessary for the missile race with the Russians:

In 1861, a Texan left to join the rebels. He told his neighbors he'd return soon, that the fight would be easy "because we can lick those damyankees with broomsticks."

He returned two years later, minus a leg. His neighbors asked the tragic, bedraggled, wounded man what happened: "You said it'd be so easy, that you could lick the damyankees with broomsticks."

"We could," replied the rebel, "but the trouble was the damyankees wouldn't fight with broomsticks."

As a United States Senator, Lyndon Johnson enjoyed telling stories when they made a point. This was one that he told:

During the early days of the Depression, a poor schoolteacher in search of a job applied to a school board. The board was rather impressed by his presentation. He was eloquent, he was factual, he was impressive. So the members of the school board said to him, "Well, we think we would like to have you teach and we would like to retain your services. But tell us this: there is some difference of opinion in our community about geography, and we want to know which side you're on. Do you teach that the world is round or do you teach that the world is flat?" The eloquent applicant responded immediately, "I can teach it either way."

Gentlemen, notwithstanding everything that has been said here today and the stirring statement which has been made, the Minority Leader has demonstrated that he can teach it either way.

I am not here today to do like the little boy who left the cotton patch and went over to hear a Senator speak one afternoon.

He came back about dark and his boss said, "Where have you been all afternoon?"

The little boy replied, "I've been listening to the United States Senator Joseph Weldon Bailey."

"The Senator didn't speak all afternoon?" the boss asked.

"Mighty near," the boy replied.

"What did the Senator say?"

"Boss, I don't remember. I don't recollect precisely but the general impression I got was the Senator was recommending himself most highly."

Manchester, New Hampshire
September 28, 1964

You know, there is the story of a college debater who told his roommate that an upcoming debate would be a real battle of wits. "How courageous of you," his friend said, "to go unarmed."

Speaking in New York City:

It is good to be here in this great city of New York that gave our nation the great artist of repartee whom we know as Al Smith.

Once Al Smith was making a speech in this city and a heckler yelled, "Tell them all you know, Al. It won't take long."

And Al answered, "I'll tell them all we *both* know and it won't take any longer."

Senator Lyndon Johnson told this story on the floor of the United States Senate:

It reminds me of the story of a train in our hill country that was brought to the foot of the hill and an old man said, "You'll never get it started up the hill."

It went up the hill, and as it started down the hill, he said, "You'll never get it stopped."

Addressing a U.S. Steelworkers' meeting in Pittsburgh, the President took delight in introducing a Republican Senator and a Republican Congressman, both of whom are known as Johnson critics:

This situation reminds me of that judge down in Texas during the Depression when they called him up one night, a state senator did, and said, "Judge, we just abolished your court."

The judge said, "Why did you abolish my court?"

And the state senator replied, "Well, we have to consolidate the courts for economy reasons. Yours was the last one created."

And the judge said, "You didn't do it without a hearing, did you? Who in the devil would testify that my court ought to be abolished?"

The state senator said, "The head of the bar association."

The judge said, "Let me tell you about the head of the bar association. He is a shyster lawyer and his daddy ahead of him was."

Then the state senator said, "The Mayor of the city came down and testified."

And the judge said, "Let me tell you about that mayor. He stole his way into office. He padded the ballot boxes. He counted them twice. Who else testified?"

The state senator said, "The banker."

And the judge said, "He has been charging usury rates like his daddy and his granddaddy ahead of him."

The state senator said, "Judge, I don't think we should talk any more tonight. Your blood pressure is getting up. The legislature did adjourn. Somebody did offer an amendment to abolish your court. I was kidding. No one testified against you at all. But I have fought the amendment and killed it. I thought it would make you feel better."

The judge said, "I know, but why did you make me say those things about three of the dearest friends I ever had?"

The moral of the story is that Republicans frequently say some of the ugliest things about some of the dearest friends they ever had, particularly in an election year.

A favorite Johnson story about a fellow Texas Democrat:

Senator Tom Connolly of Texas was once speaking about home and he started out talking about the beautiful piny woods of East Texas and then he moved on through the bluebonnets and out to the plains and down to the hill country to the Gulf Coast and then he got back to the piny woods and started all over again. And when he got all around the state that time, he started in again about those beautiful piny woods and the bluebonnets.

And this little old fellow rose up in the back of the room and yelled out, "The next time you pass Lubbock, how about letting me off?"

President Johnson told this story to a group of business leaders meeting with him at the White House:

I heard the story last night of a woman who telephoned her bank. She wanted to arrange for the disposal of a one-thousand-dollar bond. The clerk asked her, "Madam, is the bond for redemption or conversion?" There was a long pause and the woman said, "Well, am I talking to the First National Bank or the First Baptist Church?"

May, 1964

The goal of my Administration is to work for a greater society. I have come here today to ask your help in that work. I don't want you to answer me like the man who slept through the preacher's sermon down in my hill country. Every Sunday he would come and get in the front row and sleep all during the sermon.

Finally, the preacher got a little irritated and one Sunday he said, "All you people"—the fellow was snoring in the front row—and the preacher went on in a low voice, "All you people who want to go to heaven, please rise." Everybody stood up except the man who was asleep.

When they sat down, the preacher said in a very loud voice that was calculated to arouse him, "All of you men that want to go to hell, please stand up." The man jumped up. He looked around in back of him, he looked at his wife and she was sitting down. He looked at his grandmother and she was sitting down, at his children and they were sitting down. He looked at the preacher, somewhat frustrated, and he said, "Preacher, I don't know what it is we are voting on, but you and I seem to be the only two for it."

Thank you for your wonderful welcome. It wasn't entirely unexpected. My friend and associate, Dave Powers, told me on the way up here about one of the five O'Sullivan brothers. He had just had a terrific quarrel at home and he walked to the corner and met a friend, and he said to him, "I am so angry I am going to go out and disgrace the entire family. I am going to register Republican."

Boston, Massachusetts
October 27, 1964

I am reminded of the story that the Postmaster General told me about getting a letter from a little boy who had lost his father and whose widowed mother was having difficulty making ends meet. He wrote a letter to the Lord and said, "Dear God, Please send Mom a hundred dollars to help with the family."

The letter wound up on the Postmaster General's desk and he was quite touched by it so he took a twenty-dollar bill out of his pocket, put it in a Postmaster General's envelope, put an airmail stamp on it and sent it to the little boy.

About two weeks later, he got a letter back that said: "Dear God, Much obliged for all you have done, but we need another hundred. And if you don't mind, when you send it to Mama, please don't route it through Washington, because they deducted eighty per cent of it last time."

I was an NRA director back in the early days of the Roosevelt Administration in 1935, when we were taking kids out of boxcars who were riding the rails. We saw them getting their breakfast by culling grapefruit rinds that had been thrown in the garbage can. I knew a lot of social workers in those days and I still do. One of the finest women I ever knew, a social worker, told me that she had called on a family at mealtime not long ago. She told me the surroundings were meager. During the mealtime, she noticed that one of the many small children was not eating. When she asked the child why, the answer was "It is not my day to eat."

Shortly after he was elected Prime Minister in 1964, Britain's Harold Wilson visited Washington to confer with President Johnson. Alluding to his very close margin in the House of Commons, Mr. Wilson said, "I came here to ask for the loan of a few votes." To which the President replied:

We came in with a smaller majority than yours and look at us now. If you play your cards right, you'll be with us a long time.

Mr. Johnson showed his admiration for Prime Minister Wilson's abilities as a tough bargainer by telling this Mark Twain story.

It seems that Mark Twain was walking down a country road seeking the home of a friend named Henderson. Every time Twain asked another farmer how far it was, the farmer would reply "about a mile and a half." After Twain had asked the same question three times and got the same answer each time, he exclaimed, "Well, thank God, I'm holding my own."

Washington, D.C.
December, 1964

President Johnson has lightened many speeches with this anecdote:

A member of the Internal Revenue Service telephoned a Baptist minister one day and said: "I am reviewing the tax return of one of the members of your church and he listed a donation of two hundred dollars to the church. Can you tell me if he made the contribution?"

The minister replied: "I don't have my records in front of me, but if he didn't, he will!"

I see in the papers that Barry Goldwater and Rockefeller have decided to cut down their appearances in California. This reminded me of the fellow in Texas who said to his friend, "Earl, I am thinking of running for sheriff against Uncle Jim Wilson. What do you think?"

"Well," said his friend, "it depends on which one of you sees the most people."

"That's what I figure."

"If you see the most, Uncle Jim will win. If he sees the most, you will win."

In a campaign speech in Nashville, President Johnson told this anecodote:

A great man of Tennessee from Nashville became President of the United States. He was "Old Hickory" Andrew Jackson.

I have heard it said that on the day he died, the family pastor was talking with one of the President's closest friends. "Do you think the General will go to Heaven?" the pastor asked.

The old man thought a moment and replied, "Well, if he wants to go, who is going to stop him?"

October 9, 1964

Shortly after he became President, Lyndon Johnson surprised members of the Texas Democratic Congressional delegation by attending their weekly luncheon. At the luncheon, President Johnson told a story about the time Sam Rayburn had met with President Truman shortly after Truman had become President. According to Mr. Johnson, Rayburn told Truman:

Harry, they'll try to put you behind a wall down here. There will be people that will surround you and cut you off from any ideas but theirs. They'll try to make you think that the President is the smartest man in the world. And, Harry, you know he ain't and I know he ain't.

President Johnson added his own postscript to the story when he told the Texas Congressional Delegation:

And you all know he ain't.

Washington, D.C.
December, 1963

Speaking to the American Society of Newspaper Editors at the White House, the President said:

We had a preacher back home who dropped his notes just as he was leaving for church one time, and his dog jumped at them and tore them up. When the preacher went into the pulpit he apologized to his congregation and said, "I am very sorry. Today I have no sermon. I will just have to speak as the Lord directs. But I will try to do better next Sunday."

I don't have a speech today. I just intend to do as George Reedy [Press Secretary] directed at the press conference this morning—to speak as the Lord directs.

April 17, 1964

SENATOR AND
VICE PRESIDENT

Barry Goldwater is an amateur photographer and on one occasion photographed Lyndon Johnson. The Johnson photo hung in Mr. Goldwater's Senate office and was inscribed:

To Barry Goldwater from his favorite target Lyndon B. Johnson.

1961

After he lost the Democratic Presidential nomination to John F. Kennedy, Lyndon Johnson proudly pointed to the button on his lapel and said:

Someone asked me this morning what LBJ on the Johnson lapel button means. And I said, "Let's Back Jack."

Los Angeles, California
July, 1960

When Vice Presidential candidate Lyndon Johnson returned to Texas after the 1960 Democratic Convention, he was greeted by enthusiastic crowds.

There have been a lot of changes since I left here. In the first place . . . ah, second place.

July, 1960

Just prior to the 1960 Democratic Convention, Lyndon Johnson was asked by a young foreign diplomat at a dinner party, "Sir, what are your real Presidential ambitions?" Johnson replied:

My highest ambition of all is to help elect some other man President, in the hope that maybe he would make me his appointments secretary.

Once, while he was pushing a bill as Senate Minority Leader, while Senator Taft as Majority Leader was heading the opposition and receiving the bulk of the newspaper coverage, Senator Johnson telephoned a close friend who was then the Senate correspondent for a large newspaper.

Hello, [his voice came stiffly over the telephone] this is Lyndon Johnson, the Minority Leader of the Senate, you may remember. I would take it very kindly if I could have an appointment with your Senate correspondent. Now, of course, I don't want to put you out—I would be glad to meet you in Senator Taft's office.

Favorite Johnson sayings:

Any jackass can kick down a barn, but it takes a good carpenter to build one.

The best fertilizer for a piece of land is the footprints of its owner.

When you crawl out on a limb, you always have to find another one to crawl back on.

Shortly after Lyndon Johnson had his heart attack in 1955, the question arose whether he should cancel the order he had recently placed with his tailor for a blue suit and a brown one. When asked if he wanted to cancel the suits, Mr. Johnson remarked:

Let him go ahead with the blue one, we can use that no matter what happens.

Speaking of the Republicans:

I think it is very important that we have a two-party country. I am a fellow who likes small parties and the Republican party is about the size I like.

The Johnson Humor

As United States Senator, Lyndon Johnson displayed the following sign in his office:

YOU AIN'T LEARNIN' NOTHIN' WHEN YOU'RE TALKIN'.

On the eve of the Democratic Convention in Los Angeles in July, 1960, Presidential candidate Lyndon Johnson quipped:

The Vice Presidency is a good place for a young man who needs experience.

After he became Vice President, Mr. Johnson decided, on his own, that the best place for his family to live would be a Washington hotel. He went down to Washington's swank Sheraton Park Hotel and was shown a luxurious eight-room apartment. He told the hotel manager:

I like it. All I've got to do is sell Lady Bird. I used to sell hosiery door to door and if I can sell hose, I can sell Lady Bird on this.

As the hardworking Majority Leader of the Senate, Mr. Johnson had to miss many of Washington's famous parties because he was working late. One night, he arrived home very tired from the Senate. Lady Bird had just returned from a dance that he was unable to attend.

Lady Bird: I don't see why you can't take some time off for fun, Lyndon. All the others Senators do. Why, Senator Green, who is much older than you, was there and having a fine time. I danced with him twice.
Mr. Johnson: Senator Green! It was passing his pet bill through the Senate that kept me at work so late tonight.

In June, 1960, after he had announced his intention to seek the Democratic Presidential nomination, Lyndon Johnson made a political tour of New Jersey.

As I told a friend of Jack's last week, we Protestants have proven we'll vote for a Catholic. Now we want you Catholics to prove you'll vote for a Protestant.

As Vice President, Mr. Johnson visited American troops stationed in Iceland and Greenland. Reporters asked him if he was cold and uncomfortable, to which he replied:

Golly, no! We've got some of this back home in Texas. You take the Panhandle, for instance. We get hail there the size of a basketball, and the snow piles up so deep the people have to follow the jackrabbit tunnels out when the spring comes. Why, one of our boys who was up here in Greenland said that life could be a heck of a lot worse. When a gloomy roommate asked him how any place could be any worse, he answered, "Well, we could be back in Amarillo."

September, 1963

When Lyndon Johnson became Senate Majority Leader, he insisted on giving junior Senators committee assignments not based on seniority alone. When some of the senior Senators complained, Johnson told the story about a boy who had been denied a visit to a nearby city and complained that his brother had been "twowheres and I ain't been nowheres." Senator Johnson then went on to explain:

The point is that there is no sense sticking some Senators twowheres and threewheres on important committees while their capable colleagues go nowheres.

President Johnson and House Speaker Sam Rayburn were very close friends. On one occasion when he was Vice President, Mr. Johnson had this to say about Sam Rayburn:

The Speaker and I have always been very close, but if we are not as close as we were once, it is because I'm almost fifty. If you notice, he never has any old men around him.

Washington, D.C.
November, 1961

I seldom think of politics more than eighteen hours a day.

In talking about his Senate race in 1948, President Johnson said:

I won the nickname of "Landslide Lyndon" because I won by the magnificent total of 87 votes, and the Republicans have been talking about it ever since. And I've been thinking about it ever since.

Campaign Speech during tour of Midwest
October, 1964

THE PRESIDENCY

After the election returns had indicated that Johnson and Humphrey were the apparent victors of the 1964 election, President Johnson, in a speech before his campaign workers, praised Humphrey.

[He] made no mistakes and in my heart I knew he was right.

Austin, Texas
November, 1964

Speaking to a gathering of newspaper editors at the White House, the President quipped:

Ladies and gentlemen, I appreciate your coming here today. The reason I wanted you in the Rose Garden is simply because if we had gone inside the White House,

Lady Bird would have insisted that I turn on all the lights.

We are going in shortly to the White House, so you can pick up your candles in a box over there.

American Society of Newspaper Editors
April 17, 1964

On one occasion, President Johnson and his press secretary George Reedy invited the wives and children of the White House reporters to sit in on a press conference on the White House lawn.

Friends and reporters—I hope you are the same—and children of reporters. I am so glad so many of you youngsters are here today. I want to prove to you that your fathers are really on the job—sometimes. I am glad your mothers came, too. I suspect they are very pleased to find your fathers working today.

I thought you children deserved a press conference because I know that you have taken so many telephone calls for your fathers and mothers and located your wandering parents at so many receptions, that you have become good cub reporters, too.

Someone even suggested [George Reedy] you should be accredited to the White House. Here you are. I think that that person ought to remain anonymous at least until he has his hair cut again.

When the press conference is over, I want to ask all the children to come up here and pose with me for a group picture. Let's don't have any mamas or papas. They are always crowding into pictures, anyway.

May 5, 1964

Washington has changed very little since then [the New Deal era]. Not long ago I called in one of the very bright and very busy young men I have working with me, and I said to him—rather brusquely, because I was in a hurry—"The people want to know what we are going to do about the farm bill. Let's get our recommendations up right away."

He came right back and said, "Mr. President, I'll look it up, but I think you ought to tell them that if we owe it, we'll pay it."

U.S. Chamber of Commerce
April 27, 1964

At a White House dinner, the President urged a group of businessmen to help keep prices down, and promised the businessmen he was going to ask labor leaders to do the same about wages. The President went on to say:

And I will lay the cards out just as straight for them as I do for you. That way everyone will know the score —like the conversation at the card game when one of the boys looked across the table and said: "Now, Reuben, play the cards fair. I know what I dealt you."

Washington, D.C.
April 27, 1964

At a White House bill-signing ceremony, President Johnson handed one of the pens he had used to Speaker of the House John McCormack and said:

I found out that if you get along with the Speaker, you get these signing ceremonies more often. I think the Speaker works on the basis that a bill a day keeps the President away.

December, 1963

I have been giving considerable personal attention to the question of the role of the Cabinet.

The early Presidents—like Washington and Jefferson—used the Cabinet to make decisions. Lincoln fouled that up with his famous recording of a Cabinet vote as "seven noes, one aye—the ayes have it."

Washington, D.C.
January, 1965

At the swearing-in ceremony of Postmaster General John A. Gronouski:

Mr. Gronouski has stated his promise that his goal would be to provide overnight mail service to all points in the continental United States. I am for it. I would only point out that until that promise is fulfilled, I want the press to duly record that it is John Gronouski's promise, not mine. But if it does come to pass, it will be the record of the Johnson Administration.

Someone once said that the Lord made the universe and rested. The Lord made man and rested. The Lord made woman—and since then neither the Lord nor man has rested. That is what the Republican candidates found out in the New Hampshire primary when Margaret Chase Smith came on the scene.

Speaking to a group of reporters at his ranch, the President said:

You fellows know what a steer is. That's a bull who's lost his social standing.

The hardest ticket to get in Washington in January, 1965, was for President Johnson's inaugural. The President made reference to the scarcity of Inauguration tickets at the swearing-in ceremony of his new Secretary of Commerce, John T. Connor. After welcoming Connor into his Cabinet, the President said:

Before you ask me, I'll tell you. I don't have any more tickets for the Inauguration. If you find some of your business friends who do, let's split them between your relatives and mine.

Washington, D.C.
January, 1965

The President has remarked on numerous occasions that there are two kinds of speeches:

The Mother Hubbard speech which, like the garment, covers everything but touches nothing; and the French bathing suit speech which covers only the essential points.

In a campaign speech in Oregon in 1964, President Johnson told his listeners:

In 1844 a fiery young orator warned, "Make way for the young American buffalo. We'll give him Oregon for his summer shade and the region of Texas for his winter pasture."

Well, it is wonderful to be here in Oregon with you this morning. But I want it distinctly understood—I am not ready for any Texas pasture.

Speaking before a group of U.S. historians visiting Washington for the one hundred and seventieth anniversary of George Washington's inauguration, President Johnson made some gentle jibes at the reporters who were on hand.

Since the press is temporarily with us, I might explain in the words of Oscar Wilde, "In America, the President reigns for four years, and journalism governs for ever and ever."

I can assure you that at times, especially after I read the newspapers, I have strong urges to be a writer. In fact, if I may turn the tables, I sometimes think the press needs some new writers.

Washington, D.C.
May, 1964

I think that Governor Clement, who is known far and wide in this country as one of the most eloquent speakers that we have ever produced, really outdid himself in his introduction.

I honestly believe that is the second best introduction I ever had in my life. The best one was when the Governor was supposed to introduce me one time at Memphis and his legislature was in session and he didn't get to come, and I had to introduce myself.

Nashville, Tennessee
October 9, 1964

On numerous occasions in the 1964 Presidential campaign, President Johnson emphasized in his speeches the futility of any country trying to rule the world by ulti-matum. Mr. Johnson would emphasize this point by add-ing:

A long time ago down in Texas I learned that telling a man to go to hell and making him go there are two different propositions.

At a White House dance in 1964, after dancing with Peggy Goldwater, the Arizona Senator's wife, President Johnson remarked:

I have to be nice to Peggy, because I would like to be asked back here next year.

A reporter asked President Johnson if he would mind having Defense Secretary Robert McNamara as his Vice Presidential running mate, since Mr. McNamara was a former Republican. Mr. Johnson replied:

I've never been a man who believed in guilt by associa-tion.

President Johnson was asked by a reporter what his golf handicap was, and he replied:

I don't have any handicap. I am all handicap.

White House
May, 1964

The Johnson Humor

President Johnson introduced Hubert Humphrey:

. . . The man who will make the best Vice President since Lyndon Johnson.

November, 1964

President Johnson invited newsmen to watch him accept a season baseball pass from American League President Joe Cronin. After receiving the pass, President Johnson gave a pitcher's windup and announced that his arm was in fine shape to throw out the first ball of the season.

Mr. Johnson: I've got a good arm. I'm an old first baseman.
A Reporter: Lefthanded?
Mr. Johnson: No, right. I wouldn't want to do anything imprudent.

White House
April, 1964

The Johnson Humor

At the inauguration of James McCrocklin as president of Southwest Texas State College, Mr. Johnson said:

I like this inauguration so much, I think I'll have one of my own.

San Marcos, Texas
November, 1964

From a campaign speech:

We must constantly be deliberate, prudent and restrained before we shoot from the hip.

As Mr. Rayburn, the great political leader, used to say, the three most important words in the English language for everyone are: "Just a minute."

Akron, Ohio
October, 1964

*At a Democratic Party rally in Washington's National
Guard Armory, the President quipped:*

This is not a partisan dinner. It is open to any member
of any political party who wants to contribute one hundred dollars to the Democratic Party in November.

June, 1964

President Johnson was invited to address the famous Alfalfa Club at one of their dinners in Washington. New York's Governor Nelson Rockefeller had also been invited to the dinner and arrived with George Champion, chairman of the Chase Manhattan Bank. The President made reference to Mr. Rockefeller's presence with these remarks:

I'm glad that Governor Rockefeller has come here with —as they say—the friend he has at Chase Manhattan.

After he had made front-page news by lifting his dogs Him and Her by the ears, President Johnson was asked to repeat his performance for cameramen. A reporter pointed out to the President that Him had not yelped. The President replied:

He doesn't yelp unless an AP photographer gets too close to him.

The President went on to remark:

Day after I picked up that beagle by the ears, I picked him up again and I said to him, "Now, don't you yelp or those reporter fellows will quote you."

May, 1964

Pointing to the cattle-loading pens on his LBJ Ranch, Mr. Johnson said:

That's where the cattle go out and the money comes in.

During a grueling negotiation in the 1964 railroad dispute, the President made every effort to get labor and management to compromise. After a strong appeal, one of the management men remarked to Mr. Johnson, "I'm just an old country boy."
The President replied:

Hold it, stop right there. When I hear that around this town, I put my hand on my billfold. Don't start that with me.

Washington, D.C.

Accepting a forty-pound turkey for Thanksgiving from the National Turkey Foundation shortly after the 1964 election, President Johnson remarked:

I wasn't quite sure what I would eat for Thanksgiving, but I'm glad it's turkey and not crow.

November, 1964

At a St. Patrick's Day dinner in New York City, the President joked:

I woke up this morning and suddenly realized that the Irish have taken over the government and I like it.

The Speaker of the House of Representatives is a distinguished Irishman from Boston named John McCormack. And wherever I turn all day long, there are Kenny O'Donnell and Larry O'Brien and Dave Powers and George Reedy—the White House chapter of the Friendly Sons of St. Patrick.

March 17, 1964

President Johnson is aware of the fact that when he addresses a gathering of businessmen, he is not usually talking to a pro-Democratic group. Concluding a speech before a group of businessmen in Washington, the President remarked:

I must get back to your work at the White House and, I guess, let you get back to your work on me.

April 27, 1964

When President Johnson received his gold pass for the 1964 baseball season, he quipped:

Down in Johnson City, Texas, in the old days, they used to call me FBJ—First Base Johnson.

Before an early-morning press conference at the LBJ Ranch:

First, I'm glad to see so many of you made the bus this morning. When we set this early hour last evening, I asked

George Reedy [Press Secretary] if he thought the Eastern press would interpret this as extremism. He assured me that the press regards moderation in the pursuit of Eastern Daylight deadlines as no virtue.

August 9, 1964

Greeting a group of foreign students on the White House lawn:

A great American, Robert Frost, once said that you never know what a young man's chances in life are going to be until you know the kind of thing for which he will neglect his studies.

Since all of you seem to have neglected your studies to come to the White House, I think your chances are pretty good.

May 5, 1964

A Republican-inspired campaign to collect pennies to help pay the White House light bill has so far netted $1.50. That's about the way most Republican campaigns operate.

Washington, D.C.
May 20, 1964

Speaking at the opening of the New York World's Fair, Mr. Johnson turned to the president of the Fair, Robert Moses, and made these remarks:

I understand that at the close of this Fair, a time capsule will be placed in the ground. Every possible precaution has been taken to make sure that it will be opened several thousand years from now. Special metals have been used, records of its location will be stored around the world. They have neglected only one vital precaution. They do not have an advance commitment from Robert Moses that when the time finally comes, he will let them dig it up.

And now I take leave of what Odgen Nash has called "The Promised Land of Mr. Moses."

April 22, 1964

Speaking of Barry Goldwater during the 1964 Presidential campaign:

He wants to repeal the present and veto the future.

Cleveland, Ohio
October 8, 1964

At a White House ceremony honoring Pentagon employees who had contributed to the Defense Department's cost-reduction program, Mr. Johnson remarked:

Secretary of Defense McNamara is under instructions to watch costs closely these days, but I will use what influence I have to see that this hour is not charged against your annual leave.

July 21, 1964

At the swearing-in ceremony of United States Attorney General Katzenbach and Deputy Attorney General Clark, the President began the ceremony by remarking that in his part of the country there was a saying:

A town that can't support one lawyer can always support two.

Washington, D.C.
February 13, 1965

In 1790, the nation which had fought a revolution against taxation without representation discovered that some of its citizens weren't much happier about taxation with representation.

U.S. Coast Guard Academy
New London, Connecticut
June 3, 1964

At a White House press conference, Mr. Johnson was asked if he thought there were many Republicans in the audience when he made a recent campaign speech in California.

I am sure there were a good many Republicans in the audience. I would think that with a good many people there would be some Republicans. In fact, I saw two or three folks that just looked like they were Republicans.

September 21, 1964

During the 1964 campaign, President Johnson was introduced at a dinner in New York City by New York's Republican Governor Nelson Rockefeller.

I gather that the affable Governor does not share some of his colleagues' views on immigration, or perhaps we are still free at least to immigrate between the states.

Alfred E. Smith Dinner
October 14, 1964

Before a meeting of Democratic women in Washington, the President joked about his efforts to get more women into the government. As he looked at all the women in the audience, he remarked:

For a moment I thought I was in a meeting of the Federal Employees Association. I want the male members of the Democratic Party to be assured that they always have a place in the Federal Government as long as there is no woman to fill the job.

The President went on to say that women in government have not brought about too many changes.

We have not had to install more than one powder room in each federal building. We have had to hire very few babysitters. Our bureau of husband complaints requires only three people to answer the phone—and there is more demand for male secretaries than ever before.

Mr. Johnson predicted greater opportunities for women, even the office of President:

Although I hope you will forgive me for hoping that date is still a few years off.

Washington, D.C.
April 30, 1964

The President tells the story of Magnus Johnson, a Minnesota Swede, who once served in the House of Representatives.

One day, Magnus Johnson rose in the House and declared, "What we have to do is take the bull by the tail and look the situation in the face."

At a White House ceremony awarding medals to outstanding U.S. scientists, President Johnson read a citation honoring a chemist for "fundamental investigations of the comparative biochemistry of microorganisms, for studies of the basic mechanisms of photosynthesis."
After he had read the citation, the President remarked:

And I feel I deserve a medal for being able to read that citation.

Washington, D.C.
January 13, 1964

During the 1964 campaign, Senator Wayne Morse introduced President Johnson at a political rally in Oregon. After Senator Morse had completed his brief introduction, President Johnson remarked:

When you are traveling with Wayne, you are always in for a surprise. I wish he made speeches that short in the Senate—and that good.

I am glad to come here to help you celebrate the Inauguration but in the presence of Gregory Peck, I don't know that I ought to make a speech. I came here to dance with Lady Bird and Muriel (Humphrey) and anyone who will dance with me.

Inaugural Ball
Washington, D.C.
January 21, 1965

The Johnson Humor

When Astronaut John Glenn, Jr. was promoted to a full Colonel in the Marine Corps at White House ceremonies, President Johnson quipped about Glenn's famous bathroom fall.

It's odd that a man who orbits the earth and has Congress stand in rapt attention still doesn't know how to stand up in a bathtub.

October, 1964

Daniel Garcia was a student of Lyndon Johnson's when the President was a schoolteacher. Mr. Garcia appeared on a television show in 1964 to reveal the fact that Mr. Johnson had spanked him when he was in his class.

When the President met him after his television interview, he quipped:

Hello, Daniel. I just finished watching you on TV. Tell me, does it still hurt?

Washington, D.C.
January 27, 1964

In a speech before a Southern Baptist convention, President Johnson commented on a magazine article that had reported that three of his new staff members were Protestants.

It so happens that two of the three are Catholic, unless Bill Moyers [Presidential Aide] converted those two other fellows and baptized them in a mighty big hurry.

March 25, 1964

Pointing to a pistol in a Secret Service agent's holster, the President quipped to a friend:

That pistol's no good, judge. I fired it two or three times at an armadillo yesterday and it wouldn't hit a thing.

LBJ Ranch
April, 1964

In June, 1964, President Johnson addressed a Democratic fund-raising dinner in Detroit. In the audience were Henry Ford II and Jack Gordon, president of General Motors.

I am proud and inspired and stimulated that there is a Ford in my future. And with Jack Gordon here tonight I hope there is a Chevrolet. Lady Bird and I have waited so, so long to be a two-car family.

Inaugural Ball, 1965:

Never before have so many paid so much to dance so little.

Washington, D.C.
January, 1965

Noting that he had tried for a year to persuade Walter Heller to remain chairman of his Council of Economic Advisors, Mr. Johnson remarked:

His persistence in getting out of here has caused me to reflect a little the past week about the real condition of our economy.

Washington, D.C.
November 16, 1964

President Johnson invited four hundred businessmen and bankers, traditionally Republicans, to a White House conference. The first speaker to greet the businessmen was Treasury Secretary Douglas Dillon, a Republican. Next was Commerce Secretary John T. Connor, a Republican. Third to speak was Secretary of Defense McNamara, a Republican.
The President, who had introduced each man, looked up from the podium as he was about to introduce the fourth speaker and commented:

In case any of my Democratic friends managed to sneak into this meeting, I want to point out that it's only a coincidence that the first three speakers have been Republicans.

Washington, D.C.
February, 1965

After attending four other (inaugural) balls, speaking for myself and the Secret Service, I'm glad to be here tonight. One thing you can say for the Great Society, it sure is crowded.

The Vice President and I have an agreement. He will do my talking and I will do his dancing.

Inaugural Ball
Washington, D.C.
January 20, 1965

The Secretary of Labor is in charge of finding you a job, the Secretary of the Treasury is in charge of taking half the money you make away from you, and the Attorney General is in charge of suing you for the other half.

Inaugural Ball
Washington, D.C.
January 20, 1965

A Washington official placed a call to the office of Jack Valenti, one of President Johnson's White House aides. A voice that sounded familiar but wasn't Mr. Valenti's answered the phone.

Voice: Who is this?
Mr. Johnson: Lyndon Johnson.
Voice: Excuse me, Mr. President, I didn't mean to bother you. I was just calling Jack Valenti.
Mr. Johnson: Oh, that's all right. I often take Valenti's phone calls when he's busy.

President Johnson was asked by reporters how he felt concerning a poll of newspaper editors in April, 1964, that indicated he would win reelection in November, 1964.

I hope they feel in November as they do in April.

Washington, D.C.

Press Conference, January 16, 1965.

Question: Mr. President, the other day there was a report that, on a lower level in the Administration, there was a proposal to send Peace Corps volunteers to Eastern Europe. Has that reached your attention?
President Johnson: Yes, I read it in the paper. I would say that it was lower level.

Arriving at a black-tie State Department dinner for foreign diplomats in a business suit, President Johnson joked:

I trust all of you will forgive me for appearing here tonight out of uniform. The State Department and the White House have negotiated a treaty on styles and dress—Presidents don't have to wear white ties and Ambassadors don't have to wear Texas hats.

I am quite certain as I look over this audience that never before have so many intelligent men married so many beautiful women as have the members of the diplomatic corps in Washington.

Washington, D.C.
February, 1965

Presenting the award to the Teacher of the Year for 1963:

My White House job pays more than public school systems but the tenure is less certain.

Washington, D.C.
May 4, 1964

White House Press Conference:

Question: Mr. President, are you going anywhere today?
President Johnson: Not that I know of. I don't plan to but I would not want to preclude getting out, if I got through with the matters at hand and got my desk clear. I would like to take a little walk.
Question: How far, sir?
President Johnson: As far as I could, away from here.

April 4, 1964

I want to make an important policy statement. I am unabashedly in favor of women.

Women's National Press Club
March 4, 1964

At a White House ceremony swearing in eight women for jobs in his Administration:

There are some days, all too few in number, when being President is pure pleasure. I just attended a baseball game and I returned to find my household full of my favorite kind of people.

White House
April 13, 1964

Walking with reporters around the White House lawns:

I wish we could invite you fellows in for lunch but I don't think we've got enough soup.

April 11, 1964

A funny thing happened to me on the way out to Chicago. I passed Dick Nixon coming back from Vietnam and Barry Goldwater and Nelson Rockefeller going out. Harold Stassen was trying to hitchhike a ride and Bill Scranton insisted that he didn't plan to go, but if he changed his mind, he will just walk.

Chicago, Illinois
May 3, 1964

At a White House dinner honoring Eamon de Valera, President of Ireland, Mr. Johnson remarked:

You and I have a great deal in common, not the least of which is that a lot of Irishmen vote for us and occasionally against us.

Furthermore, in our work we are surrounded by Irishmen. I've heard it said that there are more Irishmen in the White House than people. And I know that I have become an Irishman by osmosis.

May 27, 1964

Speaking at the commencement exercises of his alma mater, Johnson City High School, President Johnson remarked:

I am very happy to be here tonight. Almost as happy and surprised as I was to attend my own graduation on May 25, 1924.

I only wish the people could be here now who thought it would take me forty years to get my diploma.

Johnson City, Texas
May 29, 1964

In Atlantic City, President Johnson addressed a steelworkers' convention shortly after the 1964 Democratic Convention had been held in the same city.

Were you pleased with the results of the last Atlantic City convention? [Shouts of yes from the audience.] That's wonderful. I was a little worried at first whether they made the right choice—for Miss America.

September 23, 1964

At a White House dinner honoring President Macapagal of the Philippines shortly before the 1964 election, President Johnson remarked that he had first met the Philippine President when they were both Vice Presidents. Then Mr. Johnson went on to say:

He has since succeeded in being elected President. Needless to say, I find that example commendable.

October 5, 1964

In July, 1964, the Mormon Tabernacle Choir entertained President and Mrs. Johnson in the East Room of the White House. After they had finished performing, the President told the choir that Thomas Jefferson had once complained that problems of economy made it impossible for him to hire musicians to provide music in the White House unless he employed musicians who were also willing to work around the grounds.

The President then went on to say:

Well, we have some problems of economy, too, but if some of you would like to stay around here for a while, the choir can go to work on the South Lawn and we'll put it out to cultivation.

The President then turned to Utah's Senator Frank Moss to thank him for bringing the choir to the White House.

Senator, you may stay long enough to hear one more song. Then I want you to get back up there on the hill and pass my bills.

July 24, 1964

In Atlantic City at the 1964 Democratic Convention, President Johnson joked:

My fellow Americans, my fellow Democrats, columnists and commentators: It is wonderful to be here with you tonight, but do we need all of these lights on? Do we really need all of these lights on?

August 26, 1964

Speaking in South Gate, California, during the 1964 campaign, President Johnson quipped:

I am coming back here again after November, if you invite me. If you don't invite me, I am going to be like the little boy down in the country that didn't get the invitation to the ball. I am going to sit down and write myself one.

October 11, 1964

It is much warmer here in Springfield today than at the welcome Springfield gave its most distinguished citizen when he arrived here one hundred and twenty-seven years ago.

Shortly after that arrival, Abraham Lincoln wrote a letter to a friend. He said in that letter, and I will quote him:

"I have been spoken to by but one woman since I have been here, and should not have been by her if she could have avoided it."

I guess Mr. Lincoln didn't realize that all Springfield women are naturally shy, although if those I see here reflect their grandmothers' beauty, I can see why Lincoln was disappointed.

Springfield, Illinois
October 7, 1964

Bill Miller (the Republican Vice Presidential nominee) and I have different views on immigration. I realize that this is a melting pot and I never spend a lot of time checking up on how a man spells his name, because when I looked into my family tree, I found out that I had some Irish, some Scotch, some English, a little French, a good deal of German, and sometimes in certain counties they think "Yonnie Yohnson" has a little Swede in him.

Cleveland, Ohio
October 8, 1964

I am not an old man. I am getting a little thin on top, but I'm not eligible for a pension yet.

Louisville, Kentucky
October 9, 1964

THE FAMILY

President Johnson's cousin Oriole lives in a house pro-
vided for her by the President, a half mile down the river
from the main LBJ ranch house. One night the President
was visiting Cousin Oriole with a group of reporters.
(The President usually visited his cousin every night when
he was on the ranch.) Pointing to a white telephone by the
door, Mr. Johnson said:

Cousin Oriole, what are you doing with a White House
telephone?

Cousin Oriole: They just come and put it in 'cause you're
down here so much.

Mr. Johnson: Well, don't you pick that thing up if it rings.
Khrushchev might answer.

After Mrs. Johnson had purchased a radio station in Austin, Texas, she spent much time at the station while Congressman Johnson was in Washington. Mr. Johnson missed having Lady Bird with him in Washington and on one occasion wrote her the following note:

Dearest Lady Bird,

If you don't start writing me more often, I'm going to have you drafted into the WACS. Then you will have to write to your next of kin at least twice a month.

> Your congressman,
> Lyndon B. Johnson
> *May, 1943*

Commenting on the fact that he, Lady Bird, Luci Baines and Lynda Bird all have the same initials, Mr. Johnson said:

It's cheaper this way because we can all use the same luggage.

After reading a complimentary article about himself, President Johnson turned to an associate and remarked:

I wish my mother and father could read this. My father would enjoy it and my mother would believe it.

> *Washington, D.C.*
> *September, 1964*

When Lyndon Johnson left Washington during the war, Lady Bird stayed on to run his Congressional office. After the war, he commented:

Bird ran my office so well that I was re-elected. The Tenth District would happily have elected her over me if she had run.

The other night, my little teen-age daughter came home and said—and I don't think she was being very original—"Daddy, as an outsider, how do you feel about the human race?"

For their thirtieth wedding anniversary, President Johnson presented Lady Bird with a framed picture of "Gunsmoke's" Matt Dillon, inscribed:

To Lady Bird and my Saturday night competition.

Another thirtieth wedding anniversary gift was a white envelope with money. Inscribed on the envelope was:

For the campaign traveler—a place of your own choice.
November, 1964

President Johnson's daughter Lynda Bird accompanied him to the University of Tennessee in May, 1964 where Mr. Johnson addressed the university students. The President referred to his young daughter's presence when he said:

I've been training her for nineteen years. She's supposed to know something about how to talk to college boys. If she doesn't, it's about time she learned.

In May, 1964, former President Truman celebrated his eightieth birthday. One of those who called to wish him a happy birthday was President Johnson who said:

I wanted to call collect but Lady Bird wouldn't let me.

Thanking his hosts at the Tennessee Walking Horse National Celebration for their gifts, Vice President Johnson remarked:

It's very interesting how your thinking runs. When you think of Lady Bird, you give her a very fine walking horse. But when you think of me, you give me a forty-pound ham.

September, 1961

Speaking at a national convention of the League of Women Voters, the President introduced Lady Bird as:

My secretary of war . . . a lady who lost her salary the day I took the oath of office but who was not unemployed.
The President went on to say:
We must make more use of the talents of women in order to have a better government. But one lady, Senator Margaret Chase Smith, did misunderstand my feeling. I was talking about an echelon below my job.

Pittsburgh, Pennsylvania
April, 1964

Talking to a group of reporters on the LBJ Ranch, the President remarked that they were expecting a lot of guests for dinner but that Luci's boyfriend hadn't arrived yet, but was on the way.

Luci whispered in the President's ear and Mr. Johnson corrected himself:

I mean, *one* of her boyfriends.

December, 1963

President Johnson is fond of quoting advice that he received from his father.

One of the wisest things my daddy ever told me was that "so and so is a damn smart man, but the fool's got no sense."

My daddy told me that "if I didn't want to get shot at, I should stay off the firing lines. This is politics."

My daddy used to tell me that "the time to kill a snake is when you've got the hoe in your hands."

There was a whole stable of politicians in my family background going way back to the Republic of Texas. The smartest of them was my father. He used to say that if you couldn't come into a room full of people and right away tell who was for you or against you, you had no business in politics.

During World War I, young Lyndon Johnson was earning extra money as a shoeshine boy in a barber shop in Johnson City. He thought it would be a good idea if he advertised his shoeshine stand in the newspaper. For-

tunately, his father had just purchased a local newspaper which was being run by his mother. Lyndon Johnson talked to his mother and placed the ad in the family paper. His father didn't know about the ad until it appeared.

Years later, Lyndon Johnson told the story of how his father went around town saying, "I bought a newspaper so that my wife could advertise that my son was a boot-black."

During his early days in the White House, Mr. Johnson used to tell friends that Lady Bird always asked him when he came home from the office, "Well, what did you do for women today?"

One of President Johnson's earliest memories is of his father dragging him out of bed in the morning and saying, "Lyndon, every boy in town's got an hour's start on you." This evidently made quite an impression on Mr. Johnson for he still says it himself:

An hour late and a dollar short, that's the way I've been all my life.

Commenting about his reputation as a fast driver, Mr. Johnson once remarked:

I guess something good comes out of everything. When lightning hit Lady Bird's plane the other day on her way out to Ohio, she didn't exactly say she would quit flying altogether, but she did drive nine hours back that night and got in about two-thirty in the morning.

There is one thing good about lightning hitting my wife's plane: it put her back to riding with me again.

In Florida to attend a convention of the International Ladies Garment Workers' Union:

This message came from David Dubinsky [union president] who said that he and some of his garment workers were having a meeting and would like to see me. I wanted to see the garment workers, too. I know what I have paid for some of Lady Bird's garments.

Miami Beach, Florida
February 28, 1964

At a White House press conference, the President quipped:

At least Luci does her own speeches and she doesn't take any recommendations from anyone. I found that out the other evening when I tried to make a suggestion to her.

September 21, 1964

At a press conference during the 1964 campaign, President Johnson was asked if he was worried about the problem of overconfidence.

I don't think it exists. Once, before a very important election, my wife's car was turned over and a reporter asked her, "What was your first thought when you came to?" And she said, "I wish I had voted absentee." So we don't believe in overconfidence.

Meeting with a group of forty high school student winners of a science talent search, Mr. Johnson remarked:

My daughter Luci is very interested in science—not political science, either, although she adapts herself when necessary to it. When I told her I was going to meet you, she congratulated me. She said, "Daddy, there's nothing more 'in' than brains."

White House
March 2, 1965

President Johnson sent the following telegram to the Winchester, Virginia, Apple Festival after his daughter Luci Baines had been crowned Festival Queen:

To the people of Virginia. Intelligence reports indicate that the city of Winchester is in danger of being taken over by a new monarch. Be on the alert. I have known this ruler all her life.

She entered the world with a commanding voice and has been taking over ever since. Beware of her bewitching smile. Underneath that kid glove is a strong hand. Past experience indicates that the best way of dealing with her is with total attention and love.

[Signed] Lyndon B. Johnson
Father of the Queen
April, 1964

In October, 1964, President Johnson joined the Lady Bird Special on its campaign swing through the south.

Governor, Mr. Chairman, ladies and gentlemen: Alexandria has been chosen as the first stop of one of the greatest campaigners in America, and I am very proud to announce that I am her husband.

Tonight, I am going to catch up with her in Raleigh, North Carolina, although I know I will never really overtake her. I plan to use the Air Force jet to try to meet her in New Orleans, but Lady Bird on her train will probably beat me there. She always does. Since I don't dare try and compete with her too much, we are going separate ways tomorrow.

Alexandria, Virginia

While handing out LBJ campaign buttons in Milwaukee, the President quipped:

If some Republican jumps on you for wearing them, tell them it stands for Lady Bird Johnson.

October 30, 1964

I am glad to be here tonight in the home of my ancestors. My great grandfather, George Washington Baines, was born near Raleigh on December 29, 1809. He had the good sense to marry a beautiful Southern belle from North Carolina, Melissa Ann Butler, and for the life of me, I have never been able to understand why he left North Carolina, but I guess he just got so much religion here in the land of Billy Graham that he became a Baptist preacher in a land of Baptist preachers, and he decided to spread the good word from Alabama to Louisiana, to Arkansas and he even went into Texas. Some say that he crossed the Jordan to get there, but one side of the family claims that he left the Promised Land to do it.

Raleigh, North Carolina
October 6, 1964

Speaking at a luncheon in honor of Canadian Prime Minister Lester Pearson, Mr. Johnson remarked:

One thing the Prime Minister and I have in common. We sure outmarried ourselves.

Washington, D.C.
January, 1964